EDGE
BOOKS™

✦ INTO THE GREAT OUTDOORS ✦

ICE FISHING
For Kids

BY TYLER OMOTH

Consultant:
Craig Bihrle
North Dakota Game and Fish Department
Bismarck, North Dakota

CAPSTONE PRESS
a capstone imprint

Edge Books are published by Capstone Press,
1710 Roe Crest Drive, North Mankato, Minnesota 56003
www.capstonepub.com

Library of Congress Cataloging-in-Publication Data
Omoth, Tyler.
 Ice fishing for kids / by Tyler Omoth; consultant, Craig Bihrle.
     p. cm. – (Edge books: into the great outdoors)
 Includes bibliographical references and index.
 ISBN 978-1-4296-9903-7 (library binding)
 ISBN 978-1-62065-695-2 (paperback)
 ISBN 978-1-4765-1554-0 (ebook PDF)
1. Ice fishing–Juvenile literature. I. Bihrle, Craig. II. Title.
 SH455.45.O56 2013
 796.9083–dc23   2012019494

Editorial Credits
Brenda Haugen, editor; Gene Bentdahl, designer; Eric Gohl, media researcher;
    Kathy McColley, production specialist

Photo Credits
Alamy: Aurora Photos, 29; Capstone Studio: Karon Dubke, 7, 8, 11, 12, 14, 17,
20, 25, 26; Corbis: Bettmann, 6; Dreamstime: Alla Shcherbak, 23; Newscom:
Deutsche Presse-Agentur/Gero Breloer, cover; Shutterstock: dcwcreations, 19,
Phillip Durand, 22, Piotr Wawrzyniuk, 1, Serafima, 3, Stephen Mcsweeny, 4–5

Printed in the United States of America in Brainerd, Minnesota.
092012   006938BANGS13

TABLE OF CONTENTS

The sun shines brightly, warming you even though you sit in the middle of a frozen lake. Eight inches (20 centimeters) of ice separate your world from that of the fish. You've already caught several perch and crappies using a **jig** and a couple of other **lures**. You lower your jig into a hole in the ice one more time. You move the jig up and down slowly. You hope the motion will cause a fish to bite. Suddenly your rod tip dips sharply down toward the hole. You have a hit! It's a crappie, and it's your biggest one yet. You drop the prize crappie into your bucket with the others you've caught. With this addition, you've caught your limit for the day.

jig—a lure or natural bait that is jerked up and down while fishing; jigs sometimes look like insects

lure—a fake bait used in fishing

FACT
Many people enjoy eating crappies because these fish have a flaky, white meat. In Louisiana, the Cajun term for crappie is sac-a-lait. This term means "sack of milk," and it refers to the fish's white meat.

History

Fish have been a key part of people's diets for thousands of years. For people who lived where lakes and rivers would freeze in the winter, ice fishing was a necessity. Early American Indians chopped holes in the ice over shallow areas. They used spears to nab the fish below. In ancient times, some people used fish hooks made of animal bone. They attached these hooks to line made of animal hair. They put bait on a hook and dropped the hook into the water through a hole in the ice. Then they waited for fish to bite.

Modern ice fishing has come a long way since then. Although fishing during the winter isn't a necessity for most people, ice fishing is a popular sport. Ice **augers**, ice fishing shelters, heaters, and other gear have made it easier for **anglers** to spend a day on the ice.

auger—a tool that uses a screw mechanism to drill holes

angler—a person who fishes

For a fun-filled day of ice fishing, you need to be prepared. There are many tools that can help you catch fish and stay safe. From shelters to lures, choosing the right gear will help you make the most of your ice fishing trip.

Shelters

Just because you are fishing on ice doesn't mean you have to be cold. There is a wide variety of ice fishing shelters available. Before choosing one, do some research to decide which style will work best for you.

At one time, if you wanted a shelter on the ice you had to build it yourself. People made shelters from scraps of metal or wood. Today some anglers still choose to build their own shelters. These homemade ice houses can be simple and small. But some people build large, fancy shelters because they spend a lot of time on the ice. These shelters are like a home away from home.

Homemade ice shelters made from wood or metal tend to be strong and warm. They provide good protection in strong winds. But they are often heavy and hard to move. They also take up a lot of storage space in the off-season.

Today many ice fishers buy **portable** ice shelters. These shelters are usually lightweight and fold up. Some portable shelters are little more than shelter from the wind. Others are **insulated** for added warmth. But all of these shelters are easy to move and store.

portable—easily carried or moved
insulated—covered with a material that stops heat from escaping

9

No matter what kind of shelter you choose, keep in mind your space needs. How many people will need to fit in your shelter? What items do you plan to keep in your shelter? Heaters, seats, and a light are items many fishers include in their shelters.

Ice Fishing Rods

Ice fishing rods are often much shorter than rods used for other types of fishing. Other fishing rods are usually at least 5 feet (1.5 meters) long. The extra length helps anglers when they are casting far out into a lake or river. Ice fishing rods can be short since most ice anglers sit close to the hole. Ice fishing rods are usually between 16 and 32 inches (41 and 81 cm) long.

When choosing a rod, pick one that is comfortable for you. Make sure the rod is sensitive enough to let you know when a fish bites. The type of fish you like to catch makes a difference too. You need a medium or medium-heavy rod for large game fish, such as northern pike. For panfish, such as perch or crappie, a light or ultralight rod will help you feel gentle nibbles.

Every rod needs a reel, and for ice fishing it's pretty simple. Just about any reel that fits comfortably on your rod will work. Most ice anglers use lightweight **spinning reels**.

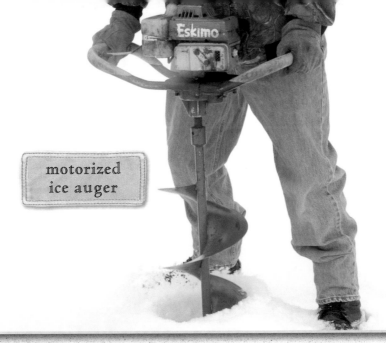

motorized
ice auger

Ice Augers

Ice makes it easy for anglers to walk to the middle of a body of water where fish are plentiful. But it also creates a barrier between the angler and the fish. Ice augers are large tools that drill holes in the ice. There are two main types of augers, manual and motorized. Manual ice augers require the user to crank a handle to turn the drill. These augers are lightweight but make getting through thick ice more difficult. Motorized augers use gas or electric engines to power the drill. They are heavier to carry than manual augers, but they make drilling a hole much easier.

spinning reel—a reel that is mounted underneath a rod instead of on top and is more sensitive to fish strikes than other rod and reel combinations

Fish Finders

Fish finders are tools that let you see how many fish are in the water below you. Fish finders also tell you how deep the fish are located. These tools can save you from hours of fishing in a spot that has no fish. They come in many models and at many different prices. For beginners, a basic model will help you find plenty of fish.

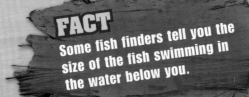

FACT
Some fish finders tell you the size of the fish swimming in the water below you.

Tip-Ups

If sitting by a hole waiting for a fish doesn't sound like much fun to you, tip-ups might be the answer. Tip-ups are tools that allow you to set your bait in the water and walk away. When the flag on your tip-up pops up, you know that you have a bite. Some people fish with two or more tip-ups at once. But check state rules to make sure you're not using more tip-ups than are allowed. Setting up tip-ups in different areas can help you find out where the fish are biting. One of the biggest advantages to using tip-ups is that they allow you to do other things. But keep in mind that tip-ups work best for larger fish that hit bait hard. Walleye and bass are fish that are often caught with tip-ups.

FISHING CONTESTS

Each year thousands of people compete in ice fishing contests. Some contests offer cash prizes based on the pounds of fish caught or for the largest fish reeled in.

The world's largest ice fishing contest is held each year in Brainerd, Minnesota. The Brainerd Lakes Ice Fishing Extravaganza has lured more than 14,000 anglers in one year. A whopping 20,000 holes are drilled for the Brainerd competition.

Many ice fishing contests, such as the one in Brainerd, are used to raise money for charities. These contests also promote the sport of ice fishing. You can find an ice fishing competition in any state that has the right winter weather for the sport.

CHAPTER 3

TIPS AND TECHNIQUES

Once you have the right equipment, it's time to get down to business. Being prepared will help you have a fun and trouble-free day. And prepared anglers usually catch more fish.

Making the Hole

Once you've found the spot where you'd like to fish, prepare your ice auger. If you have a manual ice auger, hold it straight up and down and turn the hand crank. Keep your feet a shoulder's width apart to keep your balance. Remember that ice is slippery, and augers have sharp blades. Drill the hole slowly.

Motorized augers can be a little trickier. A motorized auger is heavier than a manual auger. If you have a motorized auger, have an adult drill a hole for you.

Once you have a hole drilled, scoop out extra floating ice. As you fish, scoop out the hole once in a while to keep it from freezing over again.

Bait

If you want to catch fish, you need to have the right bait. Choose your bait based on the fish you want to catch and the technique you'll use.

Jigging works well for many fish, especially panfish. When jigging, you can usually use something simple, such as wax worms or grubs. Twister tails added to the hook on your jig can add movement and get a fish's attention. Bring a variety of different colored jigs and other lures. Fish are attracted to different colors in various water conditions. Having a variety of lures to choose from will increase your chances of catching fish.

If you want to land bigger fish, especially with tip-ups, minnows are your best bet. Game fish are **aggressive** hunters that go after smaller fish. They are more interested in minnows than wax worms or grubs. If you're using a tip-up, a live minnow provides movement to attract hungry fish.

aggressive—strong and forceful

Landing a Fish

Once a fish bites, you have to get it through the ice hole. If you're fishing with tip-ups, you will likely find the fish has either escaped or is solidly hooked. There's no reason to set the hook further. If you're jigging and get a strike, pull back on your rod in a quick motion to set the hook. But don't pull too hard or you'll lose the fish.

Most fish are easy to reel in and pull through the ice hole. But if you hook a big fish, you may need to let it take some line. Reel in the fish until it begins to pull away. Then let the fish take some line. Repeat that process a few times. This technique tires the fish and improves your chance of landing it.

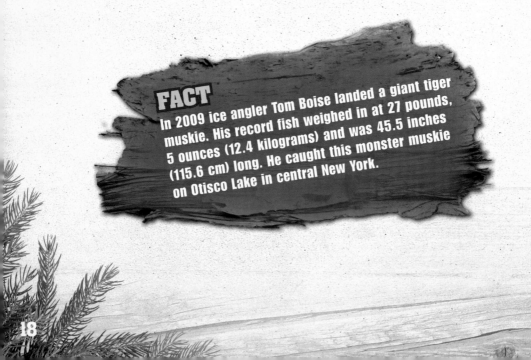

FACT
In 2009 ice angler Tom Boise landed a giant tiger muskie. His record fish weighed in at 27 pounds, 5 ounces (12.4 kilograms) and was 45.5 inches (115.6 cm) long. He caught this monster muskie on Otisco Lake in central New York.

ice picks

The first rule in ice fishing safety is don't go on the ice unless you are sure it is thick enough. Clear ice is stronger than snow-colored ice. Ice over standing water, such as in lakes, is usually sturdier than ice over running water, such as in rivers. Ice must be at least 4 inches (10 cm) thick before it's safe to walk on. Have an adult check the ice thickness with a chisel or an ice auger before deciding if it is safe.

Ice thickness can vary even in one area of a lake. Always be on your guard when you are on the ice. Check the thickness of the ice in several areas around where you want to fish. Always carry ice picks. If you fall through the ice, you can use these short stakes to grip the ice and pull yourself out of the water.

The second rule in ice fishing safety is never go on the ice alone. You should also let others know where you will be fishing.

ICE THICKNESS

Guidelines may vary a bit from state to state, but you can use the following measurements to determine when ice is safe.

2 inches (5 cm) thick or less—stay off

4 inches (10 cm)—safe for ice fishing on foot

5 inches (12.7 cm)—safe for snowmobiles

8 to 12 inches (20.3 to 30.5 cm)—safe for cars or small pickups

12 to 15 inches (30.5 to 38 cm)—safe for medium-sized pickups

Cold Weather Safety

Ice fishing is sometimes done in very cold weather. Dress for cold temperatures. You can always take off some layers of clothing if the temperature rises. It's better to have too many clothes than not enough.

For very cold days, a mask and clothing made of neoprene are important ice fishing gear. Neoprene is a rubberlike material that holds in warmth. You can also buy heat packs to put in your pockets and shoes to keep your hands and feet warm. Having the right clothing can keep you from getting **frostbite** or developing **hypothermia**.

neoprene glove

frostbite—a condition that occurs when cold temperatures freeze skin

hypothermia—a life-threatening condition that occurs when a person's body temperature falls several degrees below normal

Ice Shelter Safety

Ice shelters can make ice fishing much more enjoyable. Ice shelters keep you warm and protect you from the wind. But it's important to follow a few safety rules when using an ice shelter.

Ice should be at least 4 to 5 inches (10 to 12.7 cm) thick before you put a shelter on it. Even though some shelters are not very heavy, any extra weight can make thin ice crack.

Many anglers use propane heaters to warm their shelters. These heaters produce gas that is dangerous for you to breathe. Gas from propane heaters can cause headaches, dizziness, and even death. Your shelter should have at least two small openings where the gas can escape. If you notice some of the signs of gas poisoning, leave your shelter immediately. Then open more doors or windows in your shelter to allow more fresh air to enter. Wait a few minutes for the air to clear before going into your shelter again.

CHAPTER 5

CONSERVATION

Ice fishing is enjoyed by thousands of anglers each year. It's important to follow some basic **conservation** guidelines so the sport can continue to thrive.

Licenses

Fishing has laws that are controlled by state and federal governments. Most states let kids under a certain age fish without licenses. Make sure you purchase a license if you need one.

Limits and Catch and Release

Most states set other ice fishing rules too. Make sure you know these rules before you fish. States limit how many fish you can keep. They also have rules about the sizes of fish that anglers can keep. Fish that are too small to keep should be released as soon as possible. Also, if you catch more fish than you plan to eat, release the extras. In some states you can release fish you've kept in a bucket for a short period of time. Other states require you to release the fish right away or keep it. Releasing fish right away gives them a good chance to survive, which helps keep the fish population healthy.

CATCH AND RELEASE

If you don't plan to eat the fish you catch, you will be doing catch-and-release fishing. When catch-and-release fishing, you need to be extra careful with the fish you catch so they can be released in good condition. There are a few simple steps to catch and release that will keep the fish healthy. Special hooks without barbs on the end make it easier to unhook fish without harming them. Don't hold the fish by the gills or touch its eyes. These parts are easily damaged. Hold the fish by the mouth or sides with a gentle grip. Keep the fish in the water as much as possible and don't set it on the ice. Once the hook is freed, hold the fish in the water and gently move it back and forth until it swims away on its own power.

conservation—the protection of animals and plants, as well as the wise use of what we get from nature

Keep the Water Clean

Ice fishing would not be possible without clean water for fish to live in. When you're ice fishing, remember to leave the water as clean as it was when you arrived. Don't pour any chemicals or liquids into the water. Pick up after yourself once you've finished fishing. Once the ice melts in the spring, anything left on the ice will end up in the water and pollute it.

Just because winter covers the landscape in snow and ice doesn't mean that you need to stay inside. Get outside and enjoy ice fishing with friends and relatives. Once you get on the ice, you might be hooked for life!

MIND YOUR MANNERS

Sometimes you'll find many other anglers on the ice. When you see several anglers in one small area, it probably means that they have figured out where the fish are biting. Always ask if it's OK to fish near others before drilling your hole. Once you've settled in, respect your fishing neighbors by not being too loud. Loud noises can scare away fish.

GLOSSARY

aggressive (uh-GREH-siv)—strong and forceful

angler (ANG-glur)—a person who fishes

auger (AW-guhr)—a tool that uses a screw mechanism to drill holes

conservation (kon-sur-VAY-shuhn)—the protection of animals and plants, as well as the wise use of what we get from nature

frostbite (FRAWST-byt)—a condition that occurs when cold temperatures freeze skin

hypothermia (hye-puh-THUR-mee-uh)—a life-threatening condition that occurs when a person's body temperature falls several degrees below normal

insulated (IN-suh-lay-ted)—covered with a material that stops heat from escaping

jig (JIG)—a lure or natural bait that is jerked up and down while fishing; jigs sometimes look like insects

lure (LOOR)—a fake bait used in fishing

portable (POR-tuh-buhl)—easily carried or moved

spinning reel (SPIH-ning REEL)—a reel that is mounted underneath a rod instead of on top and is more sensitive to fish strikes than other rod and reel combinations

READ MORE

Heos, Bridget. *Ice Fishing.* Fishing: Tips and Techniques. New York: Rosen Central, 2012.

Howard, Melanie A. *Freshwater Fishing for Kids.* Into the Great Outdoors. North Mankato, Minn.: Capstone Press, 2013.

Schwartz, Tina P. *Ice Fishing.* Reel It In. New York: PowerKids Press, 2012.

INTERNET SITES

FactHound offers a safe, fun way to find Internet sites related to this book. All of the sites on FactHound have been researched by our staff.

Here's all you do:

Visit *www.facthound.com*

Type in this code: 9781429699037

 Check out projects, games and lots more at
www.capstonekids.com

INDEX